T0071515

Pianists on the recordings: [1] Brendan Fox, [2] Richard Walters

The price of this publication includes access to companion recorded piano accompaniments online, for download or for streaming, using the unique code found on the title page. Visit www.halleonard.com/mylibrary and enter the access code.

The Christmas Song
(Chestnuts Roasting on an Open Fire)

Music and Lyric by Mel Tormé
and Robert Wells
Arranged by Richard Walters

13
16
19
mf
mf
22

25
3
3
3
3
f
8va
cresc.
f
8vb
28
3
mp
mp
31
3
3
3
3
3
mf
mf
35
rit.
mp
mp
rit.
mp
p

Christmas Time Is Here

from A CHARLIE BROWN CHRISTMAS

Words by Lee Mendelson
Music by Vince Guaraldi
Arranged by Joshua Parman

19
24
f
mf
8vb
28
mp
mp
32
poco rit.
p
poco rit.

The Christmas Waltz

Words by Sammy Cahn
Music by Jule Styne
Arranged by Hank Powell

Moderate Waltz

17
21
25
29

33
37
41
Jazz Waltz
lightly
45

49
pizz.
mf
mp
54
arco
f
59
mf
mf
64

69
74
78
mp
mp
83
dim.
p

Have Yourself a Merry Little Christmas

from MEET ME IN ST. LOUIS

Words and Music by Hugh Martin
and Ralph Blane
Arranged by Celeste Avery

12
16
20
mf
cresc.
mf
23

26
rit.
a tempo
mp
rit. e dim.
mp a tempo
30
mf
mf
34
cresc.
37
dim.
f
dim.
p

The Most Wonderful Time of the Year

Words and Music by Eddie Pola
and George Wyle
Arranged by Luke Duane

Brightly, in one

16
21
1.
26
31
2.

36
(V)
cresc.
41
pizz.
p
f
p
46
arco
mp
mp
51

56
f
cresc.
f
61
66
p
cresc.
p cresc.
71
f
f

76
81
ff
ff
86
91
8va
8vb

I Wonder As I Wander
(Appalachian Carol)

By John Jacob Niles
Adapted and arranged by Celeste Avery

11
mp a tempo
13
f
f
16
mp
rit.
f
più lento
p
pp
mp
rit.
f
più lento
p

VIOLIN

CHRISTMAS SONGS
FOR CLASSICAL PLAYERS

ISBN 978-1-4950-9853-6

To access companion recorded piano accompaniments online, visit:
www.halleonard.com/mylibrary

Enter Code
7958-7933-6943-5776

Violin

The Christmas Song
(Chestnuts Roasting on an Open Fire)

Music and Lyric by Mel Tormé
and Robert Wells
Arranged by Richard Walters

Christmas Time Is Here

from A CHARLIE BROWN CHRISTMAS

Words by Lee Mendelson
Music by Vince Guaraldi
Arranged by Joshua Parman

Violin

The Christmas Waltz

Words by Sammy Cahn
Music by Jule Styne
Arranged by Hank Powell

44
5
pizz.
mf
53
58
arco
f
mf
63
68
73
78
mp
83
dim.

Have Yourself a Merry Little Christmas

from MEET ME IN ST. LOUIS

Words and Music by Hugh Martin
and Ralph Blane
Arranged by Celeste Avery

I Wonder As I Wander

(Appalachian Carol)

By John Jacob Niles
Adapted and arranged by Celeste Avery

Violin

The Most Wonderful Time of the Year

Words and Music by Eddie Pola
and George Wyle
Arranged by Luke Duane

47
arco
mp
52
57
f
62
67
p
cresc.
72
f
77
82
ff
87
92

I'll Be Home for Christmas

Words and Music by Kim Gannon
and Walter Kent
Arranged by Brendan Fox

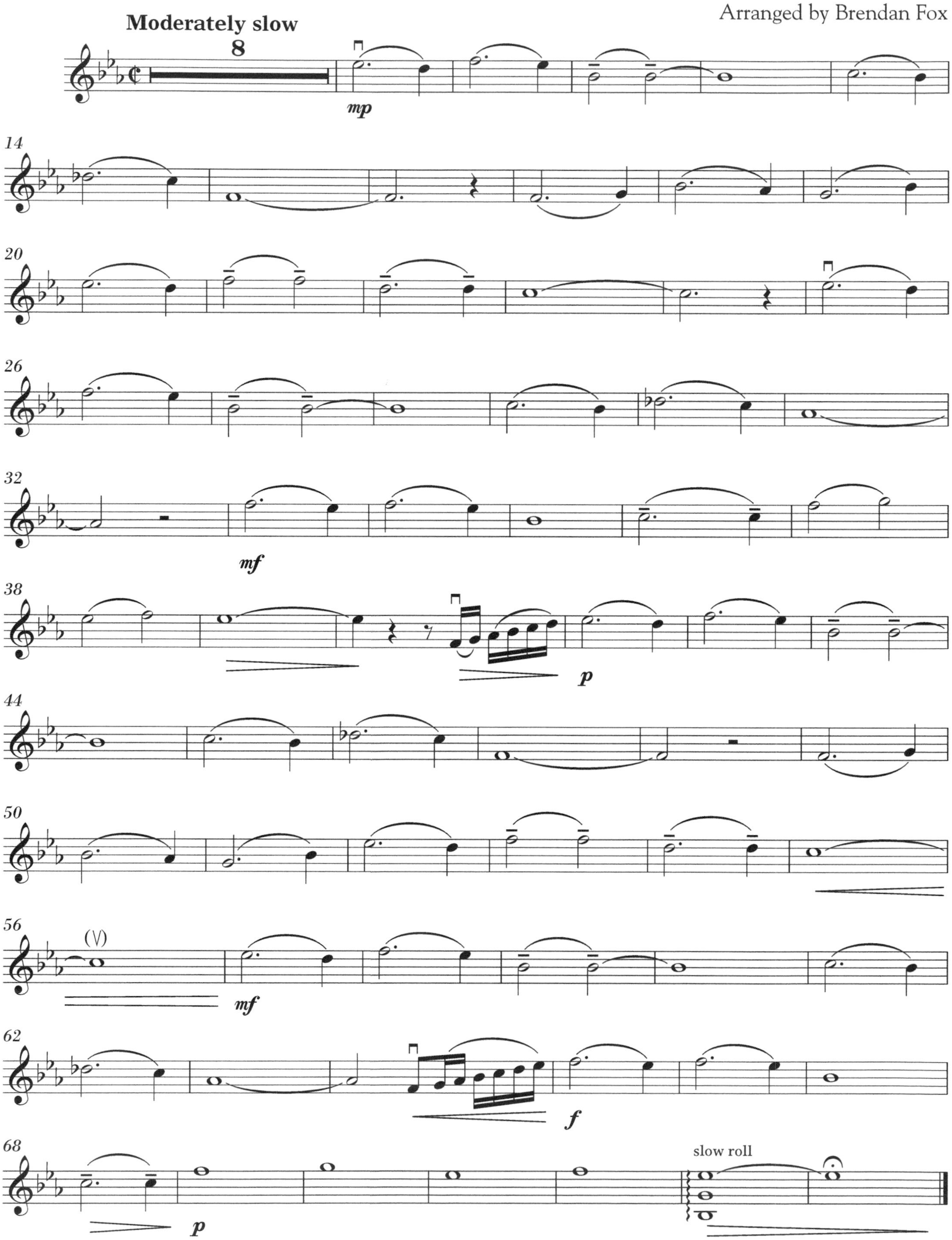

O Christmas Tree

(O Tannenbaum)

16th century Silesian folksong
Arranged by Richard Walters

Silver Bells

from the Paramount Picture THE LEMON DROP KID

Words and Music by Jay Livingston
and Ray Evans
Arranged by Luke Duane

31
36
mf
41
46
51
56
61
mp
66
p
rit.
3

Sleigh Ride

Music by Leroy Anderson
Arranged by Celeste Avery

39
43
47
To Coda
51
mp
55
f
mp
59
f
mp cresc.
63
1.
67
pizz.
arco
2.
mp cresc.
71
D.S. al Coda
CODA
dim.
p

Violin

Waltz of the Flowers

from *The Nutcracker*

Pyotr Il'yich Tchaikovsky
Arranged by Joshua Parman

Tempo di Valse

White Christmas

from the Motion Picture Irving Berlin's HOLIDAY INN

Words and Music by
Irving Berlin
Arranged by Richard Walters

19
p
21
dim.
pp
24
rit.
più lento
rit.
più lento

I'll Be Home for Christmas

Words and Music by Kim Gannon
and Walter Kent
Arranged by Brendan Fox

Moderately slow

15
20
25
30
mf
mf

35
40
p
p
45
50

55
(V)
mf
mf
60
65
f
f
p
p
70
slow roll

O Christmas Tree
(O Tannenbaum)

16th century Silesian folksong
Arranged by Richard Walters

21
mp legato
25
29
mf
8va
sub. p
pp
34
15ma

38
(15ma)
f
43
f
48
legato
53

Sleigh Ride

Music by Leroy Anderson
Arranged by Celeste Avery

16
20
24
28

32
p cresc.
mp
36
f
f
40
44

To Coda
48
51
mp
mp
55
f
mp
f
mp
59
f
mp cresc.
f
mp cresc.

63
1
mf cresc.
67
pizz.
arco
2
mp cresc.
71
D.S. al Coda
CODA
dim.
p
mf dim.
p
f

Silver Bells

from the Paramount Picture THE LEMON DROP KID

Words and Music by Jay Livingston
and Ray Evans
Arranged by Luke Duane

15
mf
p
cresc.
mf
20
p
mf
p
mf
25
p
mf
mf
p
mf
30
mf

35
mf
39
44
48
cresc.

53
f
58
mp
8va
mp
63
(8va)
p
68
rit.
p
rit.
8va

White Christmas

from the Motion Picture Irving Berlin's HOLIDAY INN

Words and Music by
Irving Berlin
Arranged by Richard Walters

13
mf
17
mp
20
24

28
32
p
p
mp
35
mf
mf
38

41
mp
44
p
mp
cresc.
f
48
mp
52
p
8va

Waltz of the Flowers

from *The Nutcracker*

Pyotr Il'yich Tchaikovsky
Arranged by Joshua Parman

20
p
p
(V)
25
mp
f
p
29
cresc.
mf
33

37
42
47
1.
52
2.